ALEXANDER HAMILTON

Copyright © 2021
University Press
All Rights Reserved

Table of Contents

Introduction
Chapter 1: From Illegitimate Birth to Orphaned Child
Chapter 2: Business at Home Leads to Education Abroad
Chapter 3: The Revolutionary War
Chapter 4: Finding Honor as a Lawyer
Chapter 5: Hammering Out and Ratifying the Constitution
Chapter 6: The Federalist Papers
Chapter 7: First Secretary of the Treasury
Chapter 8: The Panic of 1792
Chapter 9: Jefferson's 21 Objections
Chapter 10: John Jay's Treaty
Chapter 11: Hamilton and the First Political Party
Chapter 12: Hamilton's "Whiskey" Tax
Chapter 13: The New Nation's First Major Sex Scandal
Chapter 14: Contributions in the Quasi-War
Chapter 15: Hamilton's Feud with Aaron Burr
Chapter 16: Honor Above All and a Deadly Duel
Conclusion

Introduction

Alexander Hamilton could easily have been a nobody. His birth as the illegitimate son of a Scottish merchant and a woman who had left her husband gave no clue he would one day be one of the most prominent leaders of a revolution, a new nation, and a new political party. Yet, Hamilton rose from the lower social strata to become a social and political success.

Alexander Hamilton was on his way to becoming one of the Founding Fathers of America at a time when he could just as easily have spent his days begging for coins; to be an orphan in those days often meant a life of deprivation and loss. Alexander was no stranger to loss, but there was something in the boy that set him apart from his peers. Not only was he a genius, but he also had a fierce commitment to honor that would shape his destiny.

As America's first Secretary of the Treasury, Hamilton wanted the new country to be faithful in paying its debts in order to improve its reputation in the world. Later, a scandalous love affair threatened to steal the dignity he had worked so hard to achieve. Yet, he still lived nobly for the rest of his days, ending his life in a deadly duel - one last salute to his guiding principle.

Chapter 1

From Illegitimate Birth to Orphaned Child

Alexander Hamilton started life with no claims to social status. No record of his birth has ever been found, but according to a later document, he was born in 1755. Hamilton said he was born in 1757 and celebrated his birthday on January 11. He was born on the Caribbean island of Nevis and was the illegitimate son of a Scottish merchant and a woman who was married to another man.

At the time he was born, no one would have ever imagined the life he would later lead and the prominence he would gain far away from Nevis in the emerging nation of the United States. Nevertheless, as he would demonstrate over and over again, Alexander Hamilton was a person far beyond the ordinary.

Alexander's mother, Rachel Faucette Levin, was married to Johann Levin when she left her husband, her oldest son, and her home to start anew. She met and began a relationship with James Hamilton, a merchant who was often later referred to as a traveling peddler.

Although his mother was of British and French Huguenot descent and his father came from Scottish nobility, his contemporary critics claimed he was a mulatto – a person of both black and white racial heritage. Modern historians debate whether this characterization of Hamilton's descent is accurate, although enlightened people of the 21st century may wonder why being of mixed race should have been a criticism.

Living on Nevis, Alexander was exposed to many barbaric events and customs. He was appalled at slavery and horrified that a slave could have his hand cut off as punishment for theft. He also took special note of an infamous duel in which a man named Barber killed his opponent before the man had time to touch his weapon. This began his fascination with duels.

Without doubt, an illegitimate child like Alexander, born in the 18th century, would have had to endure much scorn and humiliation. While many would have let the emotional turmoil undo them, Alexander decided early on that he deserved to be treated better and someday would get the admiration and respect he should have been given as a child.

Rachel and James had two children: James Jr. and Alexander. Nine years after she left her husband, he began divorce proceedings. Alexander was ten years old when James left Rachel, ostensibly because he did not want her to be accused of adultery or bigamy. Whatever the real reason was that James deserted the family, the bottom line was that it left Rachel alone to support her children on her own.

Rachel opened a shop, where she made the young Alexander a clerk. In this position, Alexander first dealt with money and began to learn how to manage commerce and the cash it could bring. They were not rich, but the store did provide them with enough financial security to maintain the household.

Alexander's young life took another turn when his mother contracted a fever and died in 1768. Thirteen-year-old Alexander was left to fend for himself on Nevis, where life was rough, partly due to the minor criminals sent to the island by Britain. At this point, it would have been easy for Alexander to turn to a life of petty crime.

However, his natural intelligence, along with business experience as his mother's store clerk, had prepared him for a better life.

Chapter 2

Business at Home Leads to Education Abroad

Probate court left Alexander with nothing to start life on his own except a small library of 34 books. A cousin adopted him and his brother James, Jr. However, that brief respite from being an orphan ended when the cousin committed suicide. Left alone, Alexander and his brother went their separate ways.

Alexander moved to St. Croix to support himself with a job as a clerk at an import-export company that traded with New England. Alexander was so reliable and gifted in the arts of business that his employer left the youth in charge while he went away to do business elsewhere for five months. During that time, Alexander kept meticulous records and wrote to the owner to inform him of details about the business. When the owner returned, he was astonished to find that Alexander had increased his profits and broadened his customer base.

The import-export shop owner was not only grateful for Alexander's faithful service to the company, but he was also impressed by the young man's natural business acumen. The then 17-year-old Alexander wrote an essay describing the effects of a hurricane that had struck the Caribbean. The essay was published in the local paper and made a positive impression on the leaders of the community. His employer and other members of the community decided Alexander had earned a place among the educated people of the world. The community raised funds and arranged for Alexander to study in the American colonies.

Earlier, when he was a child in Nevis, Alexander was denied entry into the church-run schools because of his illegitimate birth. He received what little education he got on the island from a small independent school and learned what he could from its Jewish teachers. He so appreciated their care and devotion to their classes that he later championed the rights of Jews in America.

Once Alexander got to the American colonies, he started grammar school at the Elizabethtown Academy in New Jersey. He quickly showed the teachers there his intellectual prowess. In 1773, he went on to King's College, now called Columbia University, in New York City. He became an official student there in 1774.

Alexander excelled in his studies. Several intellectuals and visionaries of the revolution ahead took notice of him. One of these, William Livingston, took him in for a short time and taught Alexander about the reasons America should become a separate nation apart from British rule. At King's College, Alexander spoke publicly about the need for a revolution. Classmates and professors alike were impressed with his fervor and eloquence. His speaking ability even allowed him to save the college president from an angry mob. The college president was a Loyalist, but Alexander did not condone the mob's attack on him. He distracted the crowd while his college's leader escaped.

It was during his time at King's College that Alexander began his political writings. When Samuel Seabury of the Church of England wrote about reasons for staying loyal to Britain, Alexander replied with a series of writings refuting those reasons and promoting the cause of liberty.

Alexander learned quickly on his own, so he saw no need to finish his college education. He left King's College in 1776, anxious to win the fame he felt he deserved. Having learned, written, and spoken about the need for revolution, Alexander was more than prepared to join the fight for freedom.

Chapter 3

The Revolutionary War

Alexander Hamilton was set on being an important figure in the Revolutionary War; he wasted little time rising in the ranks of the Continental Army. A year after joining as a captain in early 1776, he had attained the rank of lieutenant colonel. He was also George Washington's aide-de-camp and one of the leader's closest advisors.

As aide-de-camp, Alexander penned Washington's letters to the Continental Congress, the states, and military officers. He also wrote many of the speeches Washington gave to unite the colonists and rally the army towards victory.

During this same period, Alexander began to form specific ideas of how the government should run. He, as well as Washington himself, was frustrated by the seeming inability of Congress to accomplish anything of value for the new country. He wrote letters, essays, and pamphlets privately for distribution to the public and to congress.

Although Washington relied on Alexander mainly for his intelligent ideas, visionary approach, and eloquent writing, the general also sent him on military missions. After completing these missions, he was prepared for the job of contributing to Washington's restructuring of the army. He wrote a detailed report on conditions in the field and possible ways of strengthening the army.

Sitting at a desk all day writing documents, as important as they were, became tedious in comparison to the fray of battle that Alexander imagined. He wanted to be in on the action. He got his chance while staying with Commander General Washington at Valley Forge. He rode to Monmouth Courthouse with the general and was at his side while Washington reprimanded General Charles Lee for withdrawing from the battle.

Hamilton's winter at Valley Forge taught him that the Continental government that was in charge of the new nation was ineffective at best. Soldiers were starving and had only thin clothing to protect them from the elements. Yet, the congress members were so concerned with their own individual states that they did not move to give the soldiers what they needed to fight the war. This helped shape Hamilton's belief that the nation needed to have a strong and effective central government.

In 1779, Alexander found out about a rumor that suggested he wanted to overthrow congress and install Washington as a king or dictator. Hamilton was angry at this news because he felt everyone should know that he wanted to empower Congress, not destroy it. His close friends did know he would never want what the rumor suggested.

Alexander found out the source of the rumor and sent the man, a member of the clergy, a series of letters calling for the clergyman to retract the statement. Although the matter had no impact on Hamilton's reputation and was soon forgotten, it caused him to fall into depression for a time.

Shortly afterward, Alexander began courting Elizabeth Schuyler, the daughter of a wealthy Dutch nobleman in New York. His soon-to-be father-in-law was hesitant to let Alexander marry Elizabeth, thinking that Hamilton was an opportunist after her money. However, after spending time with Alexander and realizing he was a man of integrity, he relented and allowed the marriage.

Washington and Hamilton were close friends. Alexander even sometimes seemed to find it hard to give in to his leader's authority. In 1781, Alexander was so upset by a gentle reprimand from Washington that he resigned his position as aide-de-camp. Nevertheless, he still wanted to be involved in the revolutionary fight and was still a good friend in Washington. So, a few months later, Washington set him up as commander of a light infantry battalion. That army unit is the only unit from the Revolutionary War that is still operating now, well into the 21st century.

Hamilton's opportunity came when Commander General Washington sent him and his battalion to fight the British at Yorktown. He was to clear the redoubts and engage the enemy in battle. He did just that, and did it so well that the British surrendered their troops. Hamilton, with his wife at home and his first child on the way, left the army to take up family life and the law.

Chapter 4

Finding Honor as a Lawyer

In 1782, Alexander started studying to pass the bar exam and become a lawyer in New York. Earlier that year, Robert Morris appointed him to the position of tax collector. He had little success in that job, partly because the public was not ready to be taxed and partly because the collection agencies did nothing to help him.

Next, Hamilton's appointment to the Continental Congress gave him a chance to present his ideas about the economics and government that he felt should be practiced in Washington. He became friends with James Madison, who supported him in his quest for a more effective Congress.

He wrote and argued for amendments to the Articles of Confederation to reform Congress and strengthen the central government. However, these writings were mostly overlooked by congress members, who offered little or no support for his ideas. Frustrated with the congressional process, Hamilton left Congress to become a lawyer.

He moved his family to Wall Street, the future home of stockbrokers, financial advisors, and the New York Stock Exchange. He set up an office next door to his home and began practicing law.

Hamilton accepted any case that he believed was just, even if the person had no money to pay him. In fact, his entire law practice was based on his ethical principles and commitment to justice under the laws of the confederation of the states.

Notably, he defended former loyalists who were being tried under a New York law meant to punish those who had supported Britain during the war. Since this law contradicted the requirements of the American congress's treaty with Paris, Hamilton firmly believed it was an unjust and improper law. He was also concerned that the law was driving loyalist merchants back to Britain, weakening the financial resources of the United States.

At the same time, he was practicing law as a private citizen, Hamilton was instrumental in founding the Bank of New York. His background in commerce and his writings on economics prepared him for the task of establishing the bank, which survives today as the oldest bank in the U.S.

In addition, Hamilton was among the small group of leaders who reestablished King's College, which had been damaged and suspended during the Revolutionary War. They renamed it Columbia College.

Hamilton was still dedicated to forming a stronger central government. In the 1786 Annapolis Convention, he wrote the proposal for a Constitutional Convention. His dreams of the revolutionary leaders setting up a formidable government would soon be brought to fruition.

He won a significant victory when his defense in the Rutgers vs. Waddington case succeeded in introducing the idea that the central government laws should be considered above the laws of individual states. As is true of any lawyer, Hamilton scored both wins and losses in the courts. Yet, to Alexander, his legal practice was a complete success because he followed his conscience consistently.

Chapter 5

Hammering Out and Ratifying the Constitution

Early in 1778, the states began warming up to Hamilton's proposal for a constitutional convention when John Shays led 800 angry farmers in an armed rebellion against the Massachusetts Supreme Court. The military put an end to the uprising, but the farmers, as well as others in the states, resented the high property taxes that had led them to revolt. The Constitutional Convention convened later that spring.

Alexander Hamilton was one of the three New York delegates appointed to go to the convention. However, New York governor George Clinton opposed Hamilton's federalist views and chose two other delegates who favored states' rights to go with him. Consequently, Hamilton's votes were overridden by the other two delegates until those two decided the convention was not going in their favor and left.

Although Hamilton played only a small part in the proceedings at the convention, he did give one major speech. He suggested that members of Congress and the president should be elected to serve for the rest of their lifetimes. The only exception he gave was that if a congressman or president was guilty of inappropriate behavior in his duties, he could be replaced.

Hamilton's speech was not taken well at the convention. Most delegates complained that this would set the president up as king. Hamilton defended his plan, saying that kings are not elected and that kings cannot be removed from office for bad behavior. Still, his proposal was shot down, and the constitution was written to give limited terms to the country's executive and legislative branch leaders. He was still dissatisfied but thought that at least it was an improvement over the Articles of Confederation. Hamilton signed the document as the only New York delegate.

Hamilton was much more effective in ratifying and defending the constitution. He attended the ratifying convention in Poughkeepsie. He had recently presented his ideas for the country's government in The Federalist Papers. At the convention, he presented those thoughts in dramatic speeches that mesmerized and moved the convention towards ratification.

He and other like-minded individuals argued for ratification, while Governor George Clinton and his cohort resisted it. When Virginia ratified, New York became more motivated to ratify. Clinton gave in and agreed to ratify the constitution. Not only was Hamilton persistent in calling for ratification, but New Yorkers saw accepting the document as their best chance to have George Washington, their beloved leader, as president. Ratification by all the states was completed in 1788.

Chapter 6
The Federalist Papers

During the time Alexander Hamilton was supporting the ratification of the constitution, he, James Madison, and John Jay wrote a series of 85 essays on the proposed constitution. They published these essays in several New York publications under the pseudonym of Publius. Written from 1787 to 1788, the essays were gathered into a book that was first published in 1788 as Federalist: Essays. They have become known as The Federalist Papers and remain in use today as references for courts as well as anyone who wants to understand the U.S. government better.

Most historians believe that Hamilton wrote 51 or 52 of the essays. They put forth the federalists' vision of a strong U.S. government. The purpose of the essays was to boost support and political power for the ratification of the constitution. In some senses, the documents were written as propaganda, but they contained brilliant logical arguments to support their cause.

The Federalist was also written in answer to opponents of ratification. Those who supported stronger states' rights believed that the constitution would put their states at a disadvantage. They had had enough of monarchy and argued that the constitution supported a mere revision of kingly rule.

Hamilton, Madison, and Jay wrote about the advantages of prioritizing the national government. They argued that the constitution would hold the Union together at a time when it was threatening to fall apart. They explained that the central government, though powerful, would be limited in scope and restrained by a representative legislative branch, the power of executive veto, and the contributions of the Supreme Court in maintaining justice for all.

Hamilton wrote explicitly about the checks and balances of the three-branch system proposed. He was most interested in the executive and judicial branches and wrote about them often. His writing covered subjects as seemingly disparate as the Senate, the military, and taxation. However, with his experience in each of these types of work, Hamilton could see and express the way they impacted each other.

The Federalist essay project was Hamilton's idea. He planned it, recruited the two other writers, and supervised the publication of the essays. He wrote the first essay to be published and wrote the majority of the essays.

The essays were so well-received that when a parade was held to celebrate the ratification of the constitution, the largest float was in the shape of a ship, meant to honor Hamilton, the man of the hour. His contributions to constitutional interpretation not only made him famous at the time but also cemented his place in history as one of the seven key Founding Fathers along with George Washington, Benjamin Franklin, John Jay, James Madison, Thomas Jefferson, and John Adams.

Chapter 7

First Secretary of the Treasury

When George Washington took office as the first U.S. president in 1789, he knew who he wanted as his Secretary of the Treasury. Alexander Hamilton had spoken to him about economic policies, beginning when they were working together in the Revolutionary War. Washington saw Hamilton as a man who showed both great interest and enormous potential for handling the financial matters of the new government. What is more, Hamilton agreed with Washington on critical issues regarding the economy. Washington appointed him to the office. The Senate approved the appointment on September 11, 1789.

The country's financial system was in a sorry state when Hamilton took over the job. He began immediately by requesting information from merchants and revenue agents to establish the best method of collecting the taxes to raise revenue for the country. While he waited for this information, he began writing reports on economic policies. Congress had requested these reports, which Hamilton quickly sent to them. His first report on the public credit laid out his plans for paying off the nation's debts and funding the government.

Hamilton took the model for America's fiscal policies mainly from the British system. The Brits had a circulating currency that allowed an easy exchange for goods and services and, as was important to Hamilton, for international trade.

The establishment of industry in America was also a great motivator for Hamilton's policies. He wanted to enable industries to develop and grow, allowing all people to earn a living, whether they were rich in land or not. He felt this was the best road to prosperity in the U.S., and paper currency would make it viable.

To raise funds and bring prosperity to the new nation, Hamilton turned to monied investors. These debts could be traded as paper documents. They were the first U.S. government securities. These debts would help the country develop and would be paid back with interest. However, when it came to the nation's debts to individuals and to countries that supported the war, Hamilton was adamant that those debts be paid off at a non-discounted rate and with interest as soon as possible. He wanted people to be able to exchange their Continental notes at a one-for-one rate with the new U.S. currency.

Madison did not agree with Hamilton's ideas. He thought the people who had held Continental notes should be the difference between the discounted rate they sold them for during hard times and the amount they were worth at the time the new government paid them. Under Madison's plan, the investors who had bought them would get the discounted rate they had bought them for, along with the interest due them.

Hamilton saw the futility of trying to establish who originally held the Continental notes. He also favored the investors, whom he saw as necessary funders for the new government. Neither Hamilton and Madison nor Congress could come to an agreement. So, Secretary of State Thomas Jefferson had the two men over for a meal, where he negotiated a compromise. Hamilton's fiscal plan would be accepted as it was written to support the central government, and the new capitol building would be relocated nearer to Virginia on the Potomac. This brought the necessary votes to pass Hamilton's plan because it placated the southern states.

A significant report on manufacturing was defeated in Congress, but it explained Hamilton's ideas for America better than any other. He believed the country should establish policies that would encourage both existing and future industries to make the country a prosperous nation with employment for all who sought it.

Another report argued for establishing a U.S. mint. The coins would be set in the decimal system and made of metal. However, they would not be made of gold, which would be the standard to back up the coins. Hamilton's mint ideas were accepted, and the U.S. mint was built – one more of Hamilton's significant contributions to the government as it functions today.

In the second report on the public credit, Hamilton took on the subject of establishing a national bank. He reasoned that this bank would be a safe place to handle government money. It would help with bank regulation nationwide. The nation would have a uniform currency rather than having separate currencies in individual states. During emergencies, the bank could lend the government the funds it needed to operate. He argued that a national bank would help make the country prosperous.

Madison opposed the bank bill; in his opinion, it was unconstitutional because the document never mentioned establishing a bank. President Washington was nearly convinced to veto the bill, but he gave Alexander one last chance to defend his position. Hamilton wrote a detailed explanation, interpreting the constitution as a document that allowed the means for carrying out its provisions. The bank bill passed, Washington decided not to veto it, and Hamilton established his authority as Secretary of State.

However, Hamilton did not stay in office long after the bank bill was passed. He was discouraged at the subsequent reluctance of Congress to pay off the public debt. He left his post and returned to private life in 1795, not willing to be a party to what he saw as a policy that was unjust and would weaken the country's reputation.

Chapter 8
The Panic of 1792

During Hamilton's time as Secretary of the Treasury, Wall Street became the main center of finance and investment. When he issued the first securities of the new country, it was on Wall Street that they eventually were traded.

In the summer of 1791, speculators rushed to buy up stocks. They procured the money to buy stocks by taking large loans from banks. Hamilton was firmly set against this practice, but it seems he was unable to keep banks from making the loans. Loans became easier and easier to get, and the market for the securities was tumbling towards collapse.

A group of speculators headed by William Duer bought up government securities and banknotes. Hamilton warned Duer that he was risking his reputation and his financial future, but Duer continued to buy up stock, hoping to sell to foreign investors.

The U.S. stock market crashed for the first time in February of 1792. Duer and others like him ended up in bankruptcy, and many of them ended up in prison. The government securities Hamilton had argued for were now severely devalued.

However, Hamilton stepped in to avoid a complete stock market meltdown by creating the Sinking Fund Commission. The job of the Commission was to purchase government securities in an effort to disrupt further devaluation. In addition, Hamilton told the banks to work together, combining resources to prepare for runs on deposits.

Wall Street had its own response to the crisis. As the story goes, a group of 24 stockbrokers got together under a buttonwood tree on Wall Street and signed what became known as the Buttonwood Agreement. The document established the custom of securities only being sold by stockbrokers, which cut out the sale of stocks by auctioneers. It also set the commission rates for the brokers.

Some history buffs suggest that Hamilton leaked information about the upcoming reimbursement for Continental notes to his close friends in an early incident of insider trading. There are no historical records to prove or disprove this theory. Hamilton's elitist style may seem to suggest that he would want the most intelligent people to have the greatest resources. And the most intelligent people in Hamilton's view would have been his friends.

In the light of Hamilton's general character and commitment to honor, it seems unlikely that he would do something that is now thought of as dishonorable and is now illegal. Unless he thought it was the right thing to do, he probably would not have spoken about his policies before they were announced. It is hard to say what Hamilton considered the right way to conduct business in securities in the late 1700s.

The Republicans saw the debacle as an opportunity to throw suspicion on Hamilton and diminish his influence in the government. Thomas Jefferson was at the head of the opposition to Hamilton and spoke out against him. As always, Hamilton defended himself eloquently.

Chapter 9

Jefferson's 21 Objections

Right after the stock market crash of 1792, Thomas Jefferson set out to make Hamilton's life miserable and drive him from office. These complaints against the Hamiltonian policy were published in a newspaper called the National Gazette, owned by Jefferson's friend and translator Philip Freneu. Hamilton set up his own publication called the Gazette of the United States, a Federalist paper run by John Fenno. Jefferson and Hamilton voiced their opposition to each other, each in their respective publications.

Jefferson went directly to the top in an attempt to gain more power for himself and his party and to diminish the influence of Alexander Hamilton. He wrote a list of 21 objections to Hamilton's policies and presented it to George Washington.

Jefferson's 21 Objections called out Hamilton on issues like the size of the government's debt, the presence in the market of unscrupulous "stock-jobbers," and problems he saw with the funding of the U.S. Treasury. Jefferson worried that Hamilton's focus on manufacturing and industry would detract from the farmer's economic well-being. He even suggested there was a conspiracy in place aimed to set up the U.S. as a monarchy.

Washington, being a fair man, sent the objections directly to Hamilton to get his response. The president did not tell Hamilton the identity of the person who was making the objections. Upset that he was being accused of less than honorable behavior, Alexander melded passion with logic to form a thoughtful and eloquent rebuttal.

Hamilton first conceded that the debt was sizable, but pointed out that it had taken a large amount of funds to bankroll the Revolution. The debt, he pointed out, was not from the activities of the current administration.

He also opposed the language of the section that referred to "unscrupulous stock-jobbers." In his view, there was nothing unscrupulous about dealing in securities or even in speculating on them. He felt that these people were valuable to the economic health of the country. Although it took a few people away from doing what some might consider to be more important jobs, these stockbrokers were doing the nation a service.

Hamilton did support the idea of encouraging manufacturing and industry. However, he did not see the dissonance between having a thriving industrial nation and having a thriving agricultural sector. His vision was that large population centers in the cities would have the employment they needed to survive, and farmers would live in the outlying areas, supporting the city-dwellers with needed food and raw materials.

In one section of the 21 Objections, Jefferson complained that the people who held the Continental bonds were cheated out of their full value by Hamilton's policy of paying a one-for-one rate for the bearer of the bond rather than its original owner. Hamilton replied by saying that these were fair trades. The original owners were the ones who made the decisions to part with the bonds. If they decided later that they had made a mistake, it was their own fault.

These bond transactions tended to favor the northern states, primarily because that was where the majority of the war was fought and funded. The southern states could have been on the funding of the war if they had chosen to, even though it would have been less convenient for them to have done so. According to Hamilton, things were as they should be – the northerners who helped fund the war were the ones who should profit from the bonds.

Hamilton also objected to the idea that people in the government were trying to set up a monarchy. True, there were some discussions during the constitutional convention in which the British system of government was a subject. However, the leaders who hashed out and wrote the constitution, as well as all those who signed it, could hardly be called monarchists.

After Hamilton wrote his response to the 21 Objections and gave it to Washington, he and Jefferson continued with their newspaper clash. Hamilton publicized the fact that Freneu, the editor of Jefferson's gazette, was on the government payroll. Jefferson continued to bash Hamilton's policies. Jefferson also tried to damage Hamilton's reputation by referring to his lowly origins. He even criticized Washington for giving too much honor to a man whose origins were not honorable. Nothing could have hurt Hamilton more, but he continued to support his beliefs throughout the entire incident.

After the incident with the 21 Objections was over, Jefferson continued with his campaign to oust Hamilton from office. Through his friend, William Branch Giles, he sent a long list of resolutions to Congress accusing Hamilton of corruption in appropriating funds for foreign loans and mismanaging the office of the Secretary of the Treasury. He resolved that Congress should ask for an accounting of Hamilton's actions and financial dealings in the government. He likely assumed Alexander would not have enough time to respond, as he sent the resolutions less than two months before Congress would meet to decide them.

However, Hamilton worked quickly to defend his position. He sent 200 pages of documents and records, all detailing his fair, honest, and appropriate behavior. Congress dismissed the resolutions. Jefferson tried the same thing again, but this time the resolutions were dismissed even more quickly. In fact, James Monroe was the only Republican to vote in favor of the resolutions. Hamilton had shown his true character once again, as well as his intelligence and ability to act quickly in an urgent situation.

Chapter 10
John Jay's Treaty

Alexander Hamilton was not alone in his view that the federal government should have more power than the original states. In 1787, John Adams, John Jay, and others agreed with Hamilton that the constitution that had been written could not grant this power. They had wanted a new draft. However, they pushed for ratification anyway, since they agreed it was better than the Articles of Confederation.

These leaders, although like-minded, had not formed any formal coalition. In fact, there were no political parties in the U.S. The political party system began after members of the legislative and executive branches were faced with a difficult decision.

Relations between the U.S. and Britain were strained. The independence of the United States had not settled all the issues involved in the revolution. Britain was sending massive amounts of exports into the states but was placing high tariffs on imports from the states. Often, they simply seized American goods without paying for them. They also continued to hold several forts in the northern U.S., which they had agreed to give up in the Treaty of Paris following the war. When Britain began seizing American naval ships, sailors, and military supplies being sent to France, tensions soared between the two countries.

In 1793, during Washington's presidency, Britain was at war with France. A group that included Alexander Hamilton favored Britain, while Thomas Jefferson and others wanted to support France in the conflict. Washington, who agreed with Hamilton on many issues, including this one, sent Chief Justice John Jay on a diplomatic mission to Britain to discuss the unresolved issues.

Jay relied on Hamilton for instructions on how to approach the problem. Hamilton told him to focus on improving relations with Britain in general and trade relations specifically.

Jay had little bargaining power, but he could point to the threat that the U.S. would ally with Denmark and Sweden in their bid to remain neutral by stopping Britain from seizing U.S.

ships. The Danes and Swedes used armed force to avert British seizure. If the U.S. joined the operation, it could lead to another war between Britain and the U.S.

Although Hamilton had been instrumental in sending Jay to handle these negotiations, he stole Jay's power to negotiate. He told members of the British government that there was actually no possibility that the U.S. would take up arms with the Danes and Swedes. Jay's hands were tied.

The resulting negotiation favored the British in many ways, but it did lead to improved relations and increased trade from both sides of the Atlantic. Britain could seize any U.S. ship bound for France, as long as they paid for the goods on board. They could even take French goods from U.S. ships leaving France without paying for them. They gave up their northern posts, but many other issues remained unresolved. The British government did give the U.S. Most Favored Nation status as a result of Jay's Treaty.

The treaty was extremely unpopular in the U.S., but it propelled Hamilton further into the spotlight. Men in the government who had federalist ideals began to lean on Hamilton as a leader. The first political party was in the making, and Hamilton was at the forefront of the movement.

Chapter 11

Hamilton and the First Political Party

As Congressmen bickered over Hamilton's fiscal policies and relations with Britain, Hamilton and the other federalists were forming a cohesive group. Although Washington held essentially the same views as the group that later became the Federalist Party, he opposed political factions and did not want to head the party. Thus Hamilton became the first leader of the first political party.

Hamilton's primary concern as party leader was to ensure that state rights did not supersede the national government's authority. States would still have many rights, but in matters concerning the nation as a whole, the central government would be supreme. This view was the most central ideal of the Federalist Party.

However, there was more to the party than favoring the national government over the states.

The party took an elitist approach. They were not in favor of general elections, mainly because they feared essential decisions about who would run the government and other issues would be decided based on the whims of popularity. They wanted the most intelligent people to choose the course for the country. For the same reason, they did not want to allow widespread suffrage. The Federalists did not want open elections or even democracy in general.

In addition, the Federalist Party wanted the national government to favor Britain and increase commerce between the two countries. Hamilton, as always, spoke out in favor of commerce, industry, and manufacturing. He viewed a special relationship with Britain as a positive step in that direction.

Thomas Jefferson and James Madison opposed the Federalist Party's views and gathered support to form their own party, the Democratic-Republican Party. At the time, this party was commonly called the Republican Party, but it was not the Republican Party that existed later on. This party was committed to democracy as well as states' rights. Its founders did want general open elections and preferred an agrarian society rather than an industrialized nation.

John Adams, the second U.S. president, was the first to gain that office under the party system. As a staunch Federalist, he guided the country under that party's influence. John Adams failed to get the second term he sought, though, and the Federalist Party slowly withered away until its demise in the 1820s.

Hamilton and the Federalist Party achieved several advances in their cause. The federal government gained and has remained in a superior position over the states. The U.S. did become an industrialized nation. Britain did become one of America's closest allies, not only in commerce but in subsequent wars over the decades since then. Thus the party was successful in many ways, even though its existence was short. With Hamilton as its founder, the Federalist Party had a significant impact on the later development of the U.S. political system.

Chapter 12

Hamilton's "Whiskey" Tax

Hamilton had been the force behind combining the national debt of $54 million with the states' debt of $25 million. Now, he needed a way to fund it. By the end of 1790, he had already realized that the import duties being collected were already as high as they could feasibly be set.

Criticisms were mounting over Hamilton's handling of the debt. He was also strongly motivated by his own fiscal ideals of having a government that honored its financial commitments to its citizens and to other countries. He wanted the U.S. to have an excellent reputation around the world, and he believed that would only come when the national debt was paid.

So, he proposed a domestic tax on distilled spirits. He reasoned that liquor was a luxury that people could do without if they did not want to pay the tax on it. He felt that it was the kind of tax that would cause the least resistance from the citizens. The tax bill was passed in 1791. Although the tax was for any distilled spirits, whiskey was the most popular. The tax became known as the "Whiskey Tax."

There was only one big problem with the Whiskey Tax: Hamilton had miscalculated its impact on people in rural areas. Farmers distilled whiskey and other spirits from their surplus grains. They then sold it to increase their income or traded it to buy goods they needed, using it as if it were currency.

Farmers on the western frontier made whiskey and traded it in the east as an alternative to hauling grain over the Appalachian Mountains. Some people were even paid in whiskey, meaning that they were now subject to a sort of income tax. The rural economy could not function the same way it had before as long as Hamilton's Whiskey Tax was in effect.
Farmers living west of the Appalachians were angry about the tax since it was passed in 1791 and refused to pay it. By 1794, they were so incensed they started an open rebellion as an angry mob attacked a tax collector.

Hamilton called the farmers traitors because of their refusal to support the government and their attack on a government agent. The national government needed to act quickly to put an end to this "Whiskey Rebellion."

Hamilton felt strongly that a military solution was the only acceptable course of action. Washington mobilized the military and led them over the mountains to quell the insurgency. When Washington rode out to confront the tax evaders, Hamilton demanded to be at his side.

Hamilton felt it was only right that he should face the angry farmers since he was the one who had put the tax into place. He believed that only he could explain the reasons for the tax and the need to pay it or, if they still refused, to fight for what he considered a just cause.

However, the farmers did not fight back. When confronted by Washington and his troops, they asked for clemency. Hamilton was not satisfied. He still saw them as traitors who had caused valuable time and money to be spent for no good reason. He called for their arrest, and many of the insurgents were imprisoned.

The federal troops stayed in the western regions, but Washington and Hamilton returned to the Capitol. The public press criticized Hamilton harshly, but Alexander did not respond. After the time he had already spent in the public eye, he had already learned that popular opinion was cruel but fickle. He simply ignored these attempts to tarnish his reputation. In Hamilton's opinion, the fact that the national government had prevailed was the most important issue at play.

Chapter 13

The New Nation's First Major Sex Scandal

The Reynolds affair started shortly after Alexander Hamilton took office as Secretary of the Treasury in 1791. Although there were surely sex scandals in local communities, this one is the first that rocked the new nation. It damaged Hamilton's reputation, and it may have led to his ultimate downfall.

The affair began when a young woman named Maria Reynolds arrived at Hamilton's house to ask him for help. She explained that his position gave him the power, financial resources, and high esteem of the nation to help her. Her husband, she said, had left her with no way to support herself. He had been cruel to her during the marriage, but now that he was gone, she feared she might face even more difficult times.

Hamilton's wife was out of town visiting relatives, leaving him more vulnerable to the woman's pleas. He did not have the money she needed at his home, so he told her he would bring it to her the next day. With cash in hand, he went to her rented room to deliver the funds to her and save her from her plight.

She had promised to pay back the loan. However, when Alexander got to her room, as he later said, he saw another means for her to pay him back. Thus began the sexual relationship between Maria and Alexander.

Over the next months, Maria often sent Alexander frantic letters begging him to come to see her and to help her survive her hardships. He responded to her each time, bringing money. The romantic entanglement weighed heavy on his mind. At the same time, he did give in to it of his own free will. Several times, he encouraged his wife, Elizabeth, to visit relatives or stay with them longer while he had his trysts.

On December 15 of that same year, Maria sent an even more urgent letter than she ever had before. Her husband, James, had returned and she was terrified of what he would do to both herself and Hamilton because of the affair. Two days later, James Reynolds sent a letter to Hamilton demanding he pay Reynolds the sum of $1000 so he could start a new life, now that Hamilton had destroyed his marriage. Fearing scandal, Hamilton gave Reynolds the money.

However, Reynolds did not leave town. In fact, he continued to ask for money from Hamilton, who obliged him each time. For a while, the amounts were small – typically $30 or $40. He allowed the relationship between Hamilton and his wife to continue, knowing that he could get money from Alexander as long as it did. He quit mentioning the affair and began to simply tell him that he deserved the money because he had been such a good friend to Hamilton.

In 1792, Reynolds, who had been making money in other unscrupulous ways, was jailed for committing forgery. From his jail cell, he sent Hamilton a request for help. He believed Hamilton was in a position to have him freed. Finally, Hamilton put his foot down and refused to acquiesce. Reynolds contacted James Monroe and told him his version of the sordid affair. Reynolds also gave Monroe the letters Alexander had sent him and his wife over the last year. He never mentioned that he was extorting money from Hamilton.

James Madison was politically at odds with Hamilton, but he may have had enough respect for his position to give him a chance to defend himself privately rather than addressing it in the press. For whatever reason, Madison and two of his friends visited Hamilton, presented him with the letters, and asked for an explanation.

Hamilton candidly told the trio the entire story. From his perspective, it was a bit different from Reynolds' account. He felt he had been tricked from the beginning and used for their monetary gain. According to some historians, that is precisely what happened. Maria may have been in on the plot from the beginning and was almost certainly in on it later on.

Monroe and his friends said they understood. They made copies of the letters but assured Hamilton they would never allow them to be made public. Monroe sent the letters to Thomas Jefferson. The Republican clerk, named Beckley, may also have copied the letters.

Whether the letters came from Jefferson or Monroe, which is unlikely, or from Beckley, the most credible source, is unknown. In any case, the letters resurfaced in 1797, long after Hamilton had left office, in a pamphlet by James

Callendar. Callendar, known for digging up the most sensational stories on his political opponents, described Reynolds' version of the affair. He also accused Hamilton of being involved in the speculation and forgery scheme that landed Reynolds in prison.

Alexander, faced with a choice between telling the truth or allowing citizens to lose faith in the new nation's administration, made a daring move. He printed his own pamphlet telling his side of the affair in great detail. He was less concerned with hiding the romantic details than he was with letting the public know that he had acted honorably as the Secretary of the Treasury. His message was that, yes, he had made a human error, but he had always conducted himself properly in the office they allowed him to hold. They could rely on the government.

Elizabeth remained publicly silent for the rest of her life on the subject of the affair. Because she burned all her letters that might have contained discussions of the Reynolds debacle, no one knows exactly how she felt about it. Hamilton, on his part, begged for forgiveness and, by all accounts, remained faithful to her after the affair was over. She must have forgiven him to some extent because she worked toward building his reputation for the next 50 years, even after his death.

Maria Reynolds eventually got a divorce from James. This might have been insignificant to Hamilton except for one thing. She obtained the divorce with the help of lawyer Aaron Burr. Hamilton, who had already had several conflicts with Burr, added this to the pile of insults. The two were on-and-off friends and enemies. After the Reynolds divorce, Hamilton's animosity grew.

Chapter 14

Contributions in the Quasi-War

In 1798 and 1799, during the French Revolution, Hamilton had urged Washington to make a proclamation of neutrality. He did not want to endanger relations with Britain, the country which he favored, and from which he drew many of his fiscal policies during his time in the Treasury.

When John Adams became president, he wanted to declare war on Britain because the two countries had signed a treaty to remain allies after the American Revolution. Hamilton reasoned that the government they made the treaty with was no longer in power, so there was no need to hold to the treaty. He thought they should support Britain and stay out of the chaos in France.

Neither Washington nor Hamilton was in office at this point, but they both still had considerable influence in the government. Hamilton went behind Adams' back to convince members of the executive branch to do things his way and members of Congress to vote in favor of his vision for the country.

Nevertheless, Adams began preparing for war. At Washington's request, Adams made Alexander Hamilton the senior major general of the army. He was the inspector general of the army until the summer of 1800. Washington, although still technically the head of the army, he did not want to leave Mount Vernon unless he was needed to command troops. The acting head of the army was then Alexander Hamilton.

Hamilton tried to rally troops and supply them. Many were on the brink of mutiny because they were not being paid or receiving needed supplies. Once again, Hamilton had to deal with a congress that was unwilling to fund its troops. He asked the current Secretary of the Treasury to start taxing houses, slaves, and property other than land as a way to raise funds for the army. The Secretary was slow to act and left office soon after the request.

Washington died, so Hamilton became the actual head of the army. His job was to defend the homeland against French invasion. The conflict, which became known as the Quasi-War, eventually died down before war was ever declared. Adams disbanded the army, and Hamilton returned to private life.

Chapter 15
Hamilton's Feud with Aaron Burr

Hamilton, as head of the Federalist Party in 1800, faced a difficult task. Aaron Burr was the frontrunner in the presidential race. John Adams, the current president at the time, hated Hamilton so much that he often referred publicly to Alexander's illegitimate birth and lowly beginnings. Hamilton was not in favor of a second term for Adams.

Alexander convinced many electors to vote the way that worked best to achieve his aims. At that point, the result was going to be a Jefferson/Burr presidency. According to election rules at the time, there was no presidential/vice-presidential team to vote for. The top two winners of the election would be president and vice president, with the top vote-getter taking the top office.

As much as Hamilton disliked Jefferson, he liked Burr less. He had dealt with Burr in business matters and been in the same social circles at times. Yet, from the time he knew Burr, he had multiple reasons to resent him. Burr supported an army general who was trying to oust Washington as the leader of the Continental Army during the American Revolution. The two tended to fall on opposite sides of every major conflict. In the 1804 election, Hamilton at least managed to ensure Jefferson won the presidency.

Alexander then took a respite from political to build an estate he called "The Grange." Many people in the government and also in the private sector had grown to dislike Hamilton. In 1801, as a result of his unpopularity, his beloved first son Philip was challenged to a duel to defend Alexander's honor. Philip was shot and died shortly afterward. Alexander felt responsible and grieved for his son until his own death.

Hamilton, depressed and disheartened, turned his anger on Aaron Burr. He began campaigning for a Republican presidency in the 1804 elections despite the Federalists' preference for Burr to become the next president. He tried to influence the Federalist Party to forget about Burr as president on the grounds that the man never discussed or defended his positions and so was more dangerous to the country than Jefferson. Hamilton saw himself as an open and honest man who never did anything in the government that was deceitful, and in this, he was likely right.

After Burr was defeated, he resolved to take out his anger on Hamilton, who had worked so hard to keep him from being elected. The truth is that Hamilton had less influence in the government than he ever had before. With or without Alexander's opposition, most historians say that Burr would not have been president anyway. However, the currents of conflict between the two ran too deep to allow for objective consideration by either of them.

Hamilton also worked furiously to ensure that Burr did not gain the governorship of New York. He feared that Burr would give in to popular opinion at the time that the northern states should secede from the union. This possibility put Hamilton's entire reputation and vision for the U.S. in jeopardy. When a journalist wrote about an incident at a dinner party in which Hamilton had denigrated Burr, Burr demanded a written apology.

Alexander did write a letter but admitted that he did not remember the incident and so could not say whether he had disparaged Burr or not. Burr was not appeased. He demanded satisfaction. Hamilton, not wanting to be seen as a coward, could not give it to him. The two enemies were bound for a final showdown.

Chapter 16

Honor Above All and a Deadly Duel

Hamilton had been fascinated with duels since he had heard of an infamous one during his childhood. His son's death intensified this interest. When Burr challenged him to a duel, he was prepared to defend his honor.

Duels were not unheard of in the early 1800s. However, most people found a way to avoid them. They would concede something minor or offer a generous gift, and the problem would go away. This time, though, neither party was willing to let the matter slide. The duel was to take place on July 11, 1804, at dawn in Weehawken, New Jersey.

In a political sense, Hamilton felt he had no choice but to face Burr in the duel. His moral ideals also played a part. He did not want to be responsible for taking a life. He planned to meet

Burr honorably and throw his firearm to prevent killing him.

Hamilton chose the weapons. He left the pistols with hairspring triggers and chose more easily controlled pistols. The two counted off steps and fired at each other. Neither of the seconds could tell who fired first. At least one historian suggests that Burr fired first, and Alexander returned fire immediately as he was falling.

Hamilton's ball blasted into a tree branch over Burr's head, but Burr's aim was deadly. He shot Hamilton through the liver and diaphragm, causing extensive internal damage. Hamilton, paralyzed and mortally wounded, was taken by ferry to a friend's house across the river. He had one last visit with close friends and family before dying on July 12, 1804, at his friend John Bayard's house in Greenwich Village. He was buried in the Wall Street area of Manhattan in the Trinity Churchyard Cemetery.

Conclusion

Alexander Hamilton had an overwhelming obsession with and commitment to honor - both as a person and as a government leader.

Hamilton's decisions may not have always been wise. He certainly made a terrible error in choosing to have his affair with Maria Reynolds. However, his love of his country and his dedication to building its reputation at home and abroad prompted him to admit his error and ask for forgiveness both from his country and from his beloved wife.

Elizabeth spent the rest of her life paying homage to this great man. He is remembered as one of the nation's most notable Founding Fathers. Although he was not perfect, as no one is, in the end, Hamilton's love of honor was his defining characteristic.

Printed in Great Britain
by Amazon